Windows XP Security Guide

How to perform a clean and secure install

Robert P. Millar

R & M MILLAR HOLDINGS PTY. LTD.

PUBLISHED BY

R & M MILLAR HOLDINGS PTY. LTD.
Suite 1902, 41 Blamey Street
Kelvin Grove, QLD 4059
Australia

Trademark Information

Microsoft, Windows, and Windows XP are either registered trademarks or trademarks of Microsoft Corporation in the United States and other countries.

All other names are registered trademarks or trademarks of their respective companies.

Warning and Disclaimer

This book contains information derived from NIST Special Publication 800-69, industry best practice, and hands-on experience. Every effort has been made to make this book as complete and as accurate as possible, but no warranty or fitness is implied. The information provided is on an "as is" basis. The author and the publisher shall have neither liability nor responsibility to any person or entity with respect to any loss or damages arising from the information contained in this book.

You should always use reasonable care, including backup and other appropriate precautions, when working with computers, networks, data, and files.

About the Author

Robert P. Millar (MCSE, PMP) has over 12 years of experience in Information Technology. He has worked extensively as both a Systems Engineer and as a Project Manager for Fortune 500 companies in the financial and insurance sectors, and has successfully built and developed two IT focused organizations of his own. Robert currently travels between his residences in Australia and Japan where he enthusiastically continues to build his online and offline businesses.

Table of Content

About the Author   i

Introduction   1

A Fresh Start   3

Prepare for Installation   5

    Back Up Data Files and Configuration Settings 9

    Backup or Restore Wizard 9

    Files and Settings Transfer Wizard 13

    Third-Party Backup and Restore Utility 15

    Third-Party Remote Backup Service 15

    File Copy to Media 16

Installation Procedures   17

    Boot from CD-ROM 18

    Format the Hard Drive 20

    Installing Windows Files 24

    Initial Configuration Settings 30

Securing the New Installation   35

    Set the Default View for Control Panel 36

    Identify Service Pack Currently in Use.................................... 39

Configure a Personal Firewall 41

Connect the Computer to the Network 45

    Connect to a wired network 46

    Connect to a wireless network 46

    Connect to a dialup network 48

Activate Windows 49

Apply Updates 50

Configure the Computer for Automatic Updates 58

Additional Security Steps   **61**

Malware Protection 61

Content Filtering 63

Personal Firewall 64

Customize Default Configuration   **67**

User Accounts and Session 67

    Change User Account Password 68

    Create a New User Account 69

    Fast User Switching 70

    Secure Administrator Account 71

Disable Unneeded Networking Features 73

Disable the use of remote access tools................................. 75

Secure wireless networking 76

Configure ICS 82

Sharing Files and Folders.. 85

Restore Files and Settings   89

Backup or Restore Wizard 90

Files and Settings Transfer Wizard 91

Third-Party Backup and Restore Utility 93

Third-Party Remote Backup Service 94

File Copy to Media 94

Summary   95

Resources   97

Introduction

In today's computing environment, there are many threats to home computers, including those running Microsoft Windows XP. These threats are posed by people with many different motivations, including causing mischief and disruption, committing fraud, and performing identity theft. The most common threat against Windows based home computers is malware, such as viruses and worms. Users of home computers should ensure that they are secured properly to provide reasonable protection against threats. Accordingly, this document provides guidance to people on improving the security of their own home computers (desktops or laptops) that run Windows operating systems. The recommendations draw on a large body of industry knowledge, military, government and security community experience gained over many years of securing personal computers.

Users of Windows operating systems need to be aware of the threats that their computers face and the security protections available to protect their computers so that they can operate their computers more securely. Security protections are measures used to thwart threats. Examples of common security protections are antivirus software, password-protected user accounts, and automatic software updates and patches. Security protections cannot prevent all attacks, but they can greatly reduce the opportunities that attackers have to gain access to a computer or to damage the computer's software or information. Securing a Windows based computer effectively and maintaining its security requires a combination of security protections; if one protection fails or is ineffective against a particular threat, other protections are likely to prevent the threat from succeeding. Security protections should be updated on a regular basis because new threats occur on a regular basis.

Implementing the recommendations in this guide should help improve the overall security of Windows XP computers.

A Fresh Start

Over time, an operating system can become sluggish or unstable due to a virus infection or unsafe computing practices. Instead of trying to fix everything that ails a system, it is sometimes best to start from scratch and reinstall the operating system.

This section provides guidance and step-by-step instructions for installing Windows XP. This guide assumes that Windows XP is being installed or reinstalled on the computer, which means that all existing operating system settings, applications, and data on the computer are destroyed unless first backed up to removable media or otherwise preserved. Also, the instructions in this guide should not be used on any computer that is or will be dual booting, which means that a single computer has another operating system installed in addition to Windows XP (e.g., Linux, another version of Windows).

If the computer has been previously used, it may contain user data (e.g., e-mails, documents), application configuration settings (e.g., Web browser bookmarks), or other information that needs to be preserved before Windows XP is installed or reinstalled onto the computer. In that case, the person performing the Windows XP installation should follow a five-phase process:

1. **Prepare for the Installation.** This involves basic preparatory actions, such as gathering the software media and documentation that will be needed for the installation.

2. **Back Up Data and Configuration Files.** This focuses on the transfer of user data and configuration settings from the computer to external media, such as CD-ROMs or flash drives.

3. **Install Windows XP.** This is the actual installation of Windows XP.

4. **Secure the Computer.** This involves performing various actions to secure Windows XP, such as applying service packs and software updates.

5. **Restore Data and Configuration Files.** This causes the user data and configuration settings that were backed up during phase 2 to be transferred back to the computer.

If there is no need to preserve data and configuration settings from the existing computer, the user should omit section 2.1 (Back Up Data and Configuration Files) and 7 (Restore Data and Configuration Files).

Prepare for Installation

The first thing the user should do is perform some simple preparatory steps, as follows:

1. Determine which software applications (and versions of each) are installed on the computer. These may include Web browsers, e-mail clients, office productivity tools (e.g., word processors, spreadsheets), instant messaging software, multimedia utilities (e.g., audio and video players), graphics tools, and security software (e.g., antivirus software, personal firewall). The two primary ways of identifying the installed applications are as follows:

   A. From the Control Panel, run the Add or Remove Programs utility, Figure 2-1. It shows which software applications, security updates, and other types of programs are installed on the computer.

   B. Review the folders and icons on the Start Menu and the Desktop, in particular the All Programs shortcut on the Start Menu, to find application shortcuts listed there.

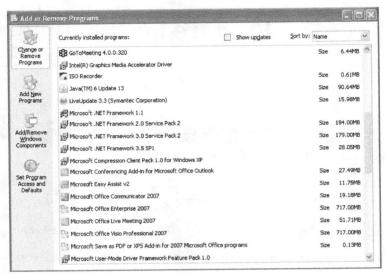

Figure 2-1 Add or Remove Programs

2. Document critical settings for the OS and applications. This should include any information needed to connect to the user's Internet Service Provider (ISP), as well as usernames or server names or addresses for applications. Examples are as follows:

✓ Network configuration information from an ISP, if the ISP does not provide this information automatically when the computer connects. Examples of network configuration information include a statically assigned IP address for the computer, default gateway IP address, and DNS server names or addresses.

✓ E-mail server names stored in e-mail clients.

✓ Usernames or nicknames used for e-mail, instant messaging programs, and other applications.

3. Gather the necessary software. This usually includes, but is not limited to, the following:

✓ Download the latest drivers for your system, e.g. network, video, audio, and wireless card.

✓ Windows XP CD and the Product Key (a series of letters and numbers in the format XXXXX-XXXXX-XXXXX-XXXXX-XXXXX)

It is important to note that some computer vendors do not provide a Windows XP CD to their customers. One common alternative is to provide a system CD that installs Windows XP and various third-party applications. Using such a system CD involves using the vendor's instructions in place of portions of the directions presented in Section 3. Some computer vendors do not provide operating system CDs with their computers; instead, the computer has software on its hard drive with which the user can create a system CD. Also, some vendors' versions of Windows XP CDs do not include Product Keys.

✓ If available, Windows XP service packs on CD.

✓ CDs, DVDs, floppy disks, and other media provided by the computer manufacturer and hardware add-on manufacturers (e.g. video drivers, sound card driver, printers, scanners, digital cameras)

✓ CDs, DVDs, floppy disks, and other media and product keys for the software applications identified in step 1 of this section. If you have the installation media, but have misplaced the product key, you may be able to recover the product key by using a key finder utility like Jalapeño Keyfinder, www.jalapenosoftware.com .

4. Gather the documentation for the computer and hardware and software added onto the computer, in case any issues arise during the installation.

5. Acquire blank writable CDs or DVDs, an external backup disk drive, or flash drives that can be used for backing up data and configuration files, if needed.

Back Up Data Files and Configuration Settings

This section describes the steps involved in backing up any information that needs to be preserved from a previously used computer. Prior to backing up any files, scan them for viruses. If the computer is new or does not contain any needed information, skip to Section 3 (Install Windows XP).

Always scan your files for viruses before backing them up.

Backup or Restore Wizard

1. By default, the backup utility is not installed with Windows XP. Before performing a backup for the first time, the user needs to load the backup utility onto the computer. This can be done using the following steps:

    A. Insert the Windows XP Home Installation CD into the CD drive.

    B. Open **My Computer**. Right-click on the CD-ROM drive and select **Explore**. Find the file located at \VALUEADD\MSFT\NTBACKUP\NTBACKUP.msi. Double-click it.

    C. The backup utility installation wizard should begin.

    D. When the wizard is complete, click **Finish**.

2. Go to **Start**, then **All Programs**, and choose **Accessories**. Next, select **System Tools**, and click on the **Backup** icon. This should launch the Backup or Restore Wizard.

3. Click the **Advanced Mode** link, Figure 2-2.

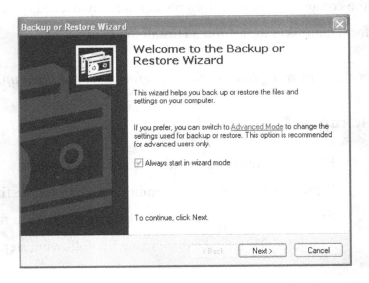

Figure 2-2 Backup or Restore Wizard

4. Click on the icon for **Backup Wizard (Advanced)**, and then click **Next,** Figure 2-3.

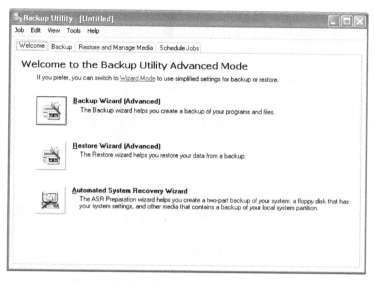

Figure 2-3Backup Wizard (Advanced)

5. The **What to Back Up** window appears, asking the user what should be backed up, Figure 2-4.

The **Back up everything on this computer** option can be used by a person logged in with an administrator account to create a backup of all users' data.

The **Back up selected files, drives, or network data** option requires someone to specify exactly which files and folders should be backed up. This option should only be used by someone who knows where all data is located.

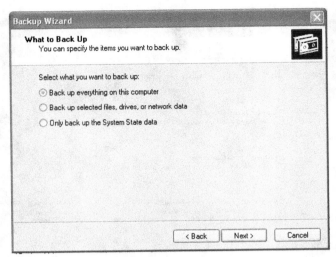

Figure 2-4 What to Back Up

The **Back up selected files, drives, or network data** option requires someone to specify exactly which files and folders should be backed up. This option should only be used by someone who knows where all data is located.

The **Only back up the System State data** option backs up the Windows Registry, system boot files, and other information that should not be transferred to the new Windows XP installation, so this backup option should not be used when rebuilding the computer.

Choose the appropriate option and click **Next**. If the **Back up selected files, drives, or network data** option was specified, then choose which data should be backed up and click **Next** when done.

6. The **Backup Type, Destination and Name** window appears. Select a place to store the backup, such as a writable CD, and specify a name for the backup. Click the **Next** button.

7. Click the **Advanced** button to specify backup options.

8. Select the **Normal** backup type, and then click the **Next** button.

9. Choose the **Verify data after backup** option, and then click the **Next** button.

10. Choose to **Replace the existing backups** and click **Next**.

11. Select **Now** to perform the backup now.

12. Confirm that the settings are correct and click the **Finish** button to start the backup.

13. Once the backup is complete, click the **Close** button.

Files and Settings Transfer Wizard

Note: This backup method is generally not preferred because it does not provide a simple way for the user to verify the integrity of the backup.

1. Click on **Start**, then **All Programs**. Choose **Accessories**, then **System Tools**. Select the **Files and Settings Transfer Wizard**, and then click **Next**.

2. Select **Old computer** to capture the current settings, Figure 2-5.

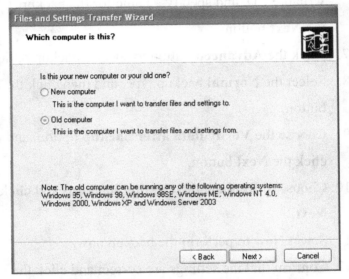

Figure 2-5 Files and Setting Transfer Wizard

3. Select **Other** and click the **Browse** button to select a location to store the files and settings to removable media, such as a CD-RW. Then click **Next**, Figure 2-6.

4. Choose to back up **Both files and settings**, then click on **Next**.

5. The wizard backs up the files and settings. Click on **Finish** when it is done. It creates a folder with a large

file (all the files and settings bundled together) and a
very small status file.

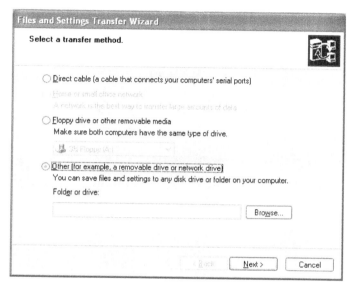

Figure 2-6 Select a transfer method screen

Third-Party Backup and Restore Utility

1. Run the utility and perform the backup based on the
   utility vendor's documentation.
2. Using features provided by the utility, verify the
   integrity of the backup.

Third-Party Remote Backup Service

1. Perform the backup using the remote backup service's
   software and directions. An example of a third party
   backup service is Carbonite, www.carbonite.com .

2. Verify the integrity of the backup using features provided by the remote backup service.

File Copy to Media

1. Select the files to be backed up, and drag them onto the media. Alternately, copy the files to be backed up, and paste them onto the media. Perform this as many times as needed to back up the files to be preserved.

2. Verify the integrity of the backup by accessing a sample of files on the media and ensuring that they are undamaged.

3. Perform an antivirus scan on the media to ensure that it does not contain any malware. Consult the antivirus software documentation for instructions on how to do this.

4. Safeguard the media. The media should be kept in a proper physical location. The media should be protected from environmental threats such as water and excess heat. Also, if needed, the media should be protected from unauthorized physical access by locking it up.

Installation Procedures

After performing any needed backups, the next step is to install Windows XP. This section provides recommendations and step-by-step instructions for doing so, focusing on the settings that have security implications. Because every computer is different, the exact steps for installing Windows XP may vary from the ones listed in this section. Users should consult their Windows XP documentation, the Microsoft Web site, or Windows XP experts whenever in doubt as to what actions to perform.

Because the computer is unsecured and vulnerable to exploitation through the internet during installation, the computer should not be connected to any network, wired or wireless, until the installation has been completed and initial security measures have been implemented.

- If the computer uses broadband (e.g., DSL, cable modem) or is part of a wired home network, disconnect the network cable from the computer that provides the network access.
- If the computer uses a wireless network, no action is necessary because the process of installing Windows

XP will effectively cause wireless networking to be unconfigured. (By default, a new installation of Windows XP will not automatically join any wireless networks.)

- If the computer uses dial-up (i.e., phone line and modem), no action is necessary because the installation process will not try to use the modem.

Boot from CD-ROM

The first part of the installation process is to load and start the Windows XP CD. This can be done using the following steps:

1. Place the Windows XP CD into the CD-ROM drive.
2. Restart the computer. A BIOS message might appear that says **Press any key to boot from CD**, Figure 3-1. If so, press any key while the message is displayed to start the boot. If the computer does not boot from the CD, then the computer might not be configured to boot from CD-ROM before other media, such as the hard drive or floppy drive. Consult the computer's hardware documentation for instructions on how to alter its BIOS settings so that the computer will boot from the CD-ROM drive before the floppy drive or hard drive. It is also possible that the Windows XP setup program does not recognize the CD-ROM drive. In that case, it may

be necessary to create a set of boot floppy disks.
Consult the vendor documentation for more information
on this.

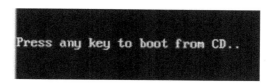

Figure 3-1 Boot from CD prompt

3. Windows Setup should open and load files. When the
   screen titled **Windows XP Setup** appears, press **Enter**
   to begin the setup, Figure 3-2.

```
Windows XP Home Edition Setup

 Welcome to Setup.

 This portion of the Setup program prepares Microsoft(R)
 Windows(R) XP to run on your computer.

     • To set up Windows XP now, press ENTER.

     • To repair a Windows XP installation using
       Recovery Console, press R.

     • To quit Setup without installing Windows XP, press F3.




 ENTER=Continue   R=Repair   F3=Quit
```

Figure 3-2Windows XP Setup Screen

4. The Windows XP Licensing Agreement should be
   displayed, Figure 3-3. Review it and press the **F8** key if
   it is acceptable.

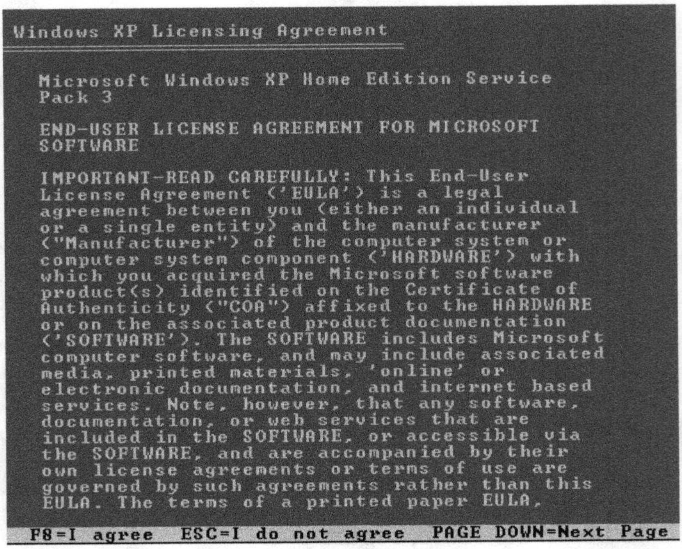

Figure 3-3 Windows XP Licensing Agreement

Format the Hard Drive

The next part of the process involves wiping out the information already on the computer's hard drive. Steps for doing this are as follows:

1. If a previous Windows XP installation is detected, the setup program will report it. Press the **Esc** key to install a new copy rather than updating the existing copy.

2. The next decision is which hard drive partition Windows XP should be loaded onto. On most computers, this is the C:\ partition. Highlight the correct partition and press **Enter,** Figure 3-4.

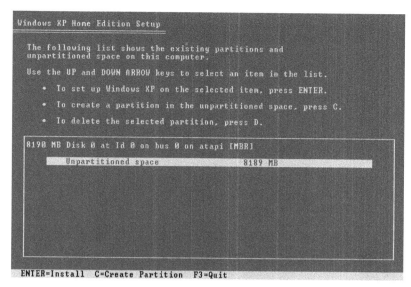

Figure 3-4 Select partition to install operating system onto

- If there are multiple old partitions from a single physical drives, these can be deleted by pressing **D**, then a new partition created by pressing **C**. Enter the maximum partition size and then press **Enter**, Figure 3-5.

- If a warning appears that there is already another operating system on the partition, confirm that the correct partition has been selected, and then press **C** to continue loading Windows XP.

3. The next decision is which file system should be used, File Allocation Table (FAT) or NT File System (NTFS). NTFS offers security features that FAT does not, so unless there is a specific reason why FAT needs

to be used, select the **Format the partition using the NTFS file system (Quick)** option and press **Enter**. If the hard drive has been in use for a while and has a lot of data on it, it might be preferable to select the **Format the partition using the NTFS file system** option (without the "Quick"), Figure 3-6.

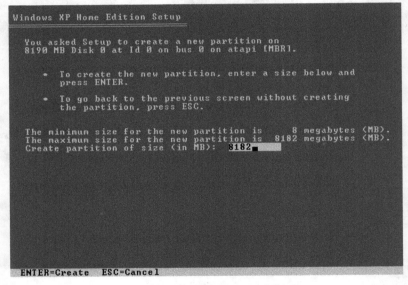

Figure 3-5 Creating a partition

3. If asked, press **F** to initiate the formatting. (This question is only displayed if the hard drive has existing data on it.)

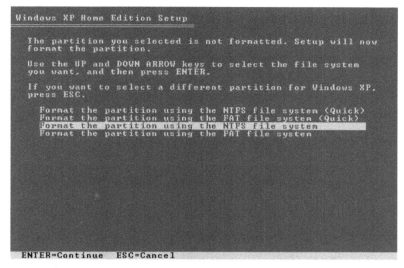

Figure 3-6 Format Partition using NTFS file system

Formatting will now begin, wiping all data from the drive. This could take between several minutes to an hour depending on the size of the hard drive, Figure 3-7.

Figure 3-7Formatting hard drive

Installing Windows Files

Once the drive has been formatted, the setup program will begin to install Windows XP onto the computer, Figure 3-8. This process could take between several minutes and a few hours, depending on the computer's hardware.

Figure 3-8 Installing Windows progress

The user is next prompted to make certain basic configuration choices, as follows:

1. The **Regional and Language Options** window appears, Figure 3-9. Make any desired changes and click **Next** when done.

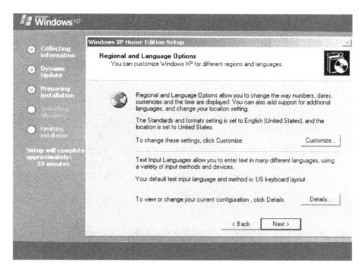

Figure 3-9 Regional and Language Options window

2. The **Personalize Your Software** window appears, Figure 3-10. A name must be entered; the organization name is optional. When done, click **Next**.

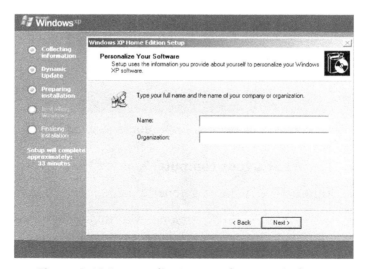

Figure 3-10 Personalize Your Software window

3. Once prompted, enter the **Product Key** (a series of
   letters and numbers in the format XXXXX-XXXXX-
   XXXXX-XXXXX-XXXXX), Figure 3-11. It is usually
   found on or with the packaging containing the
   Windows XP CD. After entering the Product Key, click
   Next. **Note**: Some vendor-specific versions of
   Windows XP may not require a product key to be
   entered, and will skip this step.

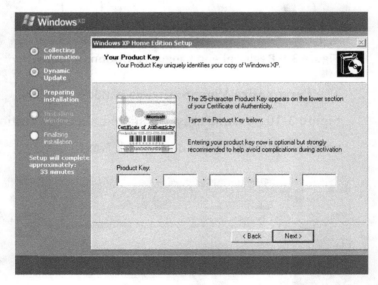

Figure 3-11 Enter Your Product Key window

4. The **What's your computer's name?** window appears,
   Figure 3-12. Type in a generic name for the computer;
   however, do not use personal information or describe
   the physical location. Do not use the automatically
   generated name. Click **Next** when done.

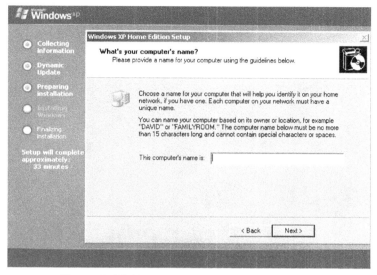

Figure 3-12 Name Your Computer screen

5. The **Modem Dialing Information** window appears
   next if Windows XP recognizes a modem in the
   computer. If so, enter the requested dialing information.
   Even if the modem is not going to be used, the area
   code still needs to be entered so that the setup process
   can continue. After doing so, click **Next**.

6. The **Date and Time Settings** window appears, Figure
   3-13. Set the correct date, time, time zone, and daylight
   saving settings. Once set, click **Next**.

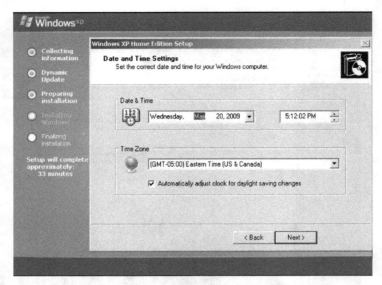

Figure 3-13 Date and Time Settings windows

7. The **Networking Settings** window appears, Figure 3-14. Select **Custom settings** and click **Next**.

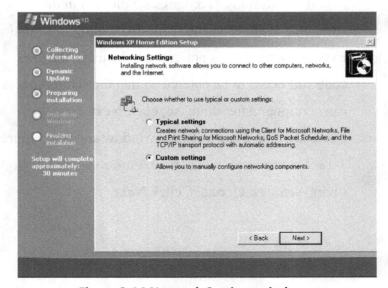

Figure 3-14 Network Settings window

8. In the **Networking Components** window Figure 3-15, unselect the check box for **QoS Packet Scheduler**. Also unselect the check box for **File and Printer Sharing for Microsoft Networks** unless this computer will be sharing its files or printers with other computers on the local network. If the computer will not be using shared folders or printers from other computers on the local network, also unselect the check box for **Client for Microsoft Networks**. When done, click on **Next**.

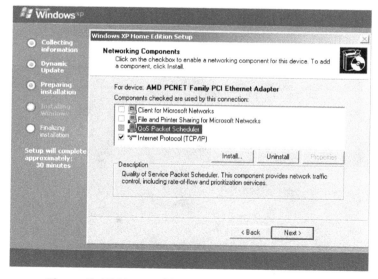

Figure 3-15 Networking Components window

Initial Configuration Settings

After the initial configuration is complete, the computer will reboot. If prompted to press a key to boot from CD, do **not** press a key. Windows XP will load. Once the reboot has been completed, additional configuration settings need to be made, as follows:

1. Click on **Next** on the Welcome to Microsoft Windows screen to start the configuration process, Figure 3-16.

2. Choose the option that reflects how the computer will first connect to the Internet, Figure 3.17.

Figure 3-16 Welcome to Microsoft Windows

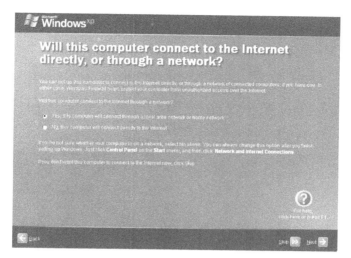

Figure 3-17 Internet Connection screen

3. The next screen prompts the user to activate Windows XP. Because the computer is not yet network-connected, activation cannot be performed at this time. Select the **No, remind me every few days** option and click on **Next**, Figure 3-18.

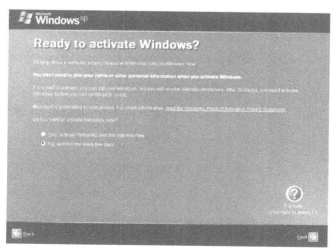

Figure 3-18 Windows Activation screen

4. If the CD included Windows XP Service Pack 2, the next screen asks if Automatic Updates should be enabled, Figure 3-19. This setting is configured later in the instructions, so at this time choose the **Not right now** option and click **Next**.

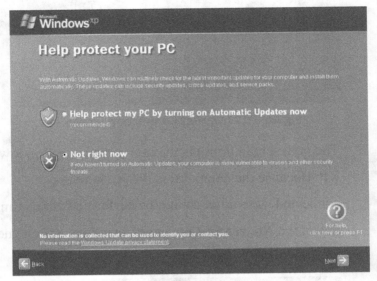

Figure 3-19 Automatic Update screen

5. At least one user account must be created during the configuration process. **Any accounts created at this time will have administrative privileges**, so only one account should be added now. Once the computer is fully secured, other accounts can be created. Enter a username for the computer's administrative account in the **Your name** box, then click **Next**, Figure 3-20.

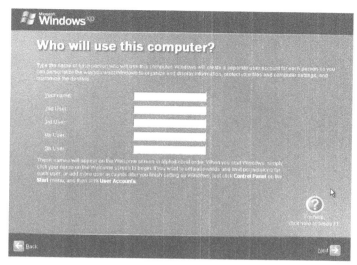

Figure 3-20 Computer Users screen

6. The installation of Windows XP is complete. Click
   Finish, Figure 3-21

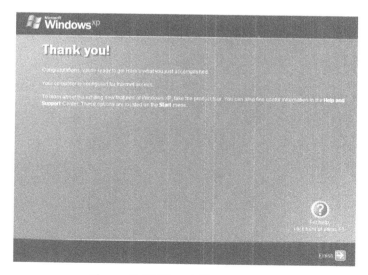

Figure 3-21 Thank You screen

Windows XP will now open with the user account that was created in the previous step, Figure 3-22.

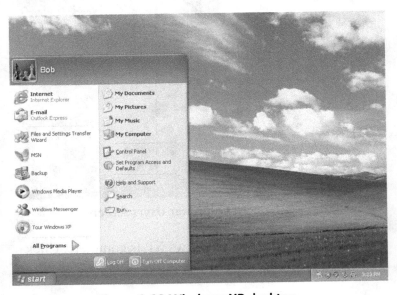

Figure 3-22 Windows XP desktop

Securing the New Installation

Before anyone uses a newly installed Windows XP computer, it should be properly secured to minimize the possibility of a security breach. This section provides guidance and step-by-step instructions for securing a new installation of Windows XP. The guidance in this section assumes that the computer has not been attached to any networks since Windows XP was installed. If the computer has been on a network, it could have already been compromised because Windows XP has only a few security features enabled by default. This section also assumes that the computer has not yet been used and does not yet contain any data.

Prior to securing the computer, gather the software media and documentation that might be needed, including the following:

- ✓ Documentation and support information from the computer's manufacturer

- ✓ Windows XP software, including the Windows XP CD and service pack CDs (if applicable)

- ✓ Software from the computer's manufacturer

✓ Software for third-party user applications, such as word
processors, graphics tools, e-mail clients, and Web
browsers

✓ Software for third-party security applications, such as
antivirus software, personal firewalls, and data
encryption utilities

✓ Serial numbers for third-party applications that may be
needed to register them.

If antivirus software and antispyware software is not already
present, it should be acquired before starting to secure the
computer. If the existing security software is significantly out
of date (generally, several years old), it should be upgraded to a
new version if possible, otherwise replaced with a new version.
For example, outdated antivirus software typically lacks newer
detection capabilities and other features that are needed to
detect and stop relatively recent malware threats.

Set the Default View for Control Panel

Control Panel has two views: Category and Classic. Category
View groups similar items together, and Classic View lists
each Control Panel item separately. The instructions in this
guide assume that Classic View is being used.

1. Click **Start**, then select the **Control Panel**, Figure 4-1.

Figure 4-1 Start menu

2. Look at the text in the upper left hand corner of the Control Panel window, Figure 4-2.

-   If it contains a link that says **Switch to Classic View**, click on that link to change the default view from Category View to Classic View.

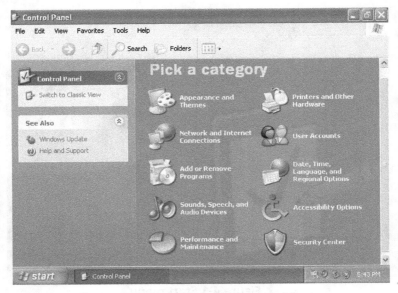

Figure 4-2 Control Panel Category View

- If it contains a link that says **Switch to Category View**, no action is needed because **Classic View** is already the default setting, Figure 4-3.

- If it does not contain either a **Switch to Category View** or a **Switch to Classic View** link, no action is needed because the Windows classic folders option is enabled, which allows only Classic View to be used.

Figure 4-3 Control Panel Classic View

Identify Service Pack Currently in Use

It is very important to determine which Windows XP service pack the computer is currently running. Certain directions in this section are specific to a particular service pack version. To identify the running service pack, perform the following steps:

1. From the **Control Panel**, double-click the **System** icon. The **System Properties** window should appear.

2. Under the **General** tab, the information displayed for the **System** should indicate which service pack is currently loaded on the computer, such as Service Pack 1, Figure 4-4, or Service Pack 2, Figure 4-5. If no

service pack is listed, then the computer does not have a service pack installed.

3. Click on **OK**.

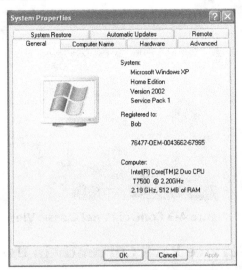

Figure 4-4 System Properties SP1

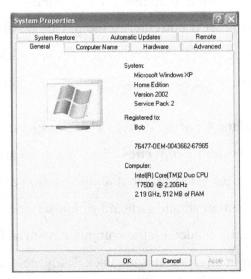

Figure 4-5 System Properties SP2

Configure a Personal Firewall

Before the computer is connected to any network to get updates, a personal firewall needs to be set up on the computer to block malicious activity from other computers, such as worms. At this point, installing antivirus software is generally not necessary. It is likely that the antivirus software media is several months out of date and will not be effective at stopping most malware threats until the computer is connected to a network and updated. Without a personal firewall enabled and configured to block unauthorized network activity, a computer connected to the Internet that has not had updates applied is typically compromised in minutes. If configured properly, a firewall router can also be effective at protecting unpatched computers during the update process. However, because firewall routers are third-party hardware devices, it is outside the scope of this document to discuss their configurations. Also, computers that are protected by firewall routers should also be protected by personal firewalls as an additional layer of defense, particularly against other computers on the same local network that may become infected with malware.

This section provides step-by-step instructions for identifying, acquiring, and applying the updates, as well as guidance on configuring a personal firewall to protect the computer during the updating process.

Until the computer has been fully updated, applications such as e-mail clients, instant messaging clients, and word processors should not be used. The only application use should be that which is required to update the computer or configure the personal firewall. Web browsers should be used only for updating the computer and not for general web surfing or other purposes.

All pre-SP2 versions of Windows XP have a built-in personal firewall called Internet Connection Firewall (ICF). ICF offers the ability to block unauthorized network activity directed at a Windows XP computer, but by default ICF is disabled. Windows XP SP2 replaces ICF with a new built-in personal firewall called Windows Firewall. By default, Windows Firewall enables itself if a third-party firewall is not already present. Many new computers contain trial versions of third-party personal firewalls, so new Windows XP computers could have two or more personal firewalls installed. This guide recommends using the built-in personal firewall and disabling all others, but users could instead use a third-party personal firewall and disable all others. Follow the appropriate set of directions below to enable and configure the built-in personal firewall to block all unnecessary activity during patching.

If the computer is using Service Pack 1 or is not using a service pack at all, perform the following steps to ensure that a personal firewall is enabled and providing adequate protection for the computer:

1. Log on to the computer using an administrative-level account.
2. If any third-party personal firewall programs are installed on the computer, refer to the software vendors' documentation and help files, and follow their directions to disable them.
3. In the **Control Panel**, double-click the **Network Connections** icon. The Network Connections configuration box should be displayed.
4. Right-click the connection that needs to be configured with ICF, then click **Properties**.
5. Select the **Advanced** tab. Enable ICF by checking the box for **Protect my computer and network by limiting or preventing access to this computer from the Internet.**
6. Click on **OK** to save the firewall configuration.

If the computer is already using SP2, perform the following steps to ensure that Windows Firewall is enabled and providing adequate protection for the computer:

1. Log on to the computer using an administrative-level account.

2. In the **Control Panel**, double-click on the **Security Center** icon.

The Security Center window should now be displayed.

3. The firewall status should indicate if a third-party firewall is enabled, Figure 4-6.

   If so, refer to the software vendors' documentation and help files, and follow their directions to disable them.

4. Check the firewall status. If it is listed as **OFF**, perform the following sub-steps:

   A. Click on the **Recommendations...** button.

   B. Turn the firewall on by clicking the **Enable now** button. A notification window should appear, saying that the firewall was enabled successfully. Click on **Close**.

Figure 4-6 Security Center window

C. Click on **OK** to close the **Recommendation** window. The firewall status should now be listed as **ON**.

5. Close the **Security Center**.

Connect the Computer to the Network

The next step is to connect the computer to a network. Networking options include telephone modems, broadband (e.g., DSL, cable modem), or a wired or wireless Local Area Network (LAN). This section provides the steps needed to set up a Windows XP computer to use each of these networking options. If the computer will use multiple forms of networking, such as a cable modem and wireless, follow each applicable set of directions below.

Connect to a wired network

If the computer uses a wired local area network or broadband (e.g., DSL, cable modem) for its access to other networks, simply connect the network cable to the computer to establish network connectivity. The DHCP server should supply the computer with the necessary information needed for network communications.

Connect to a wireless network

If the computer uses a wireless local area network, follow the steps listed below:

These instructions assume that the wireless connectivity features built into Windows XP are being used to configure and manage the wireless network card. In some cases, it may be desirable to use a separate wireless configuration utility provided by the vendor of the wireless network card, or a vendor's version of Windows XP may use such a utility by default. If a separate utility is to be used, skip the steps below and instead follow the directions from the utility's vendor on how to configure it to establish wireless network connectivity. If you are unsure if a separate utility is being used, it should become obvious after attempting a few steps of the directions whether or not these steps are correct for your situation.

1. From the **Control Panel**, double-click on the **Network Connection** icon.

2. Right-click the wireless connection that needs to be configured, then click **Properties**. (If a wireless network connection entry does not exist, the proper driver for the wireless network card may not be installed. Follow the wireless card manufacturer's directions for installing the driver.)

3. A list of wireless networks in range should be displayed (if not, select **View Wireless Networks** to display them). Select the correct wireless network and click on the **Connect** button. Note that wireless networks can be "hidden" so that their names do not appear in the list. If the network is "hidden", click the **Add** button and manually type the network's SSID (wireless network name), then click **OK** to connect.

4. If a WEP or WPA key is required by the wireless access point, enter it when requested and click on **Connect**. Section 6.4, Securing Wireless Networking, provides additional information on wireless security, including WEP and WPA keys

Connect to a dialup network

If the computer uses a telephone modem for its access to other networks, follow these steps:

1. From the **Control Panel**, double-click on the **Network Connections** icon.
2. Click on **File**, then **New Connection** to run the New Connection Wizard. When the wizard window appears, click **Next**.
3. Click on the **Connect to the Internet** option and click **Next**.
4. The user needs to choose from three options: **Choose from a list of Internet service providers (ISPs), Set up my connection manually**, and **Use the CD I got from an ISP**. Select the appropriate option based on the ISP's instructions or documentation, and click **Next**.
5. Provide all requested information and follow the prompts based on the ISP's instructions or documentation.
6. After filling in the ISP-specific information, click on **Add a shortcut to this connection to my desktop,** and then click **Finish**.

Activate Windows

Before downloading updates, Windows XP Home must be activated, because Microsoft will not allow downloading of the latest Service Packs without ensuring that a legitimate copy of Windows is being used. Activating just ensures that the version of Windows is legitimate and is not the same as registering, though registration can be accomplished at the same time.

1. Activating Windows can be accomplished in any of the following ways:

   > Begin activation when the **Activate Windows** window pops up automatically when logging in.
   > Click on **Start**, then **All Programs**, then **Accessories**, then **System Tools**. Select **Activate Windows**.
   > Click on the **Activate Windows** icon in the Quick Launch area. The icon looks like a set of keys.

2. Assuming there is a working Internet connection, click on **Yes, let's activate Windows over the Internet now**. Alternatively, activation can be performed by telephoning Microsoft customer support and following their guidance.

3. Register and click **Next**. Registration data should then be entered on the next page.

4. Activation should then complete automatically. If Windows cannot connect to the Internet, a connection screen will appear to help connect to the Internet. If activation fails, call Microsoft customer support.

Apply Updates

The next step in securing Windows XP is to apply updates to it. Although some updates may be available on CD, such as Windows XP Service Pack 2, most need to be downloaded from the Internet. If a service pack CD is available, it should be used first before downloading additional updates.

Both Automatic Updates and Microsoft Update can be used to download some updates. However, although Automatic Updates can acquire and install all Windows XP security-related updates, it does not include all updates, such as hardware drivers. The Microsoft Update Web site can be used to acquire and install all types of updates, both security and non-security-related. To use Microsoft Update, perform the steps below.

Because the predecessor to Microsoft Update was named Windows Update, Windows XP computers that are not fully updated may display "Windows Update" instead of "Microsoft Update" on some screens. This should not be a cause for concern; during the update process, Windows Update will eventually be replaced with Microsoft Update.

1. Run **Internet Explorer**.
2. Click on **Tools**, then **Windows Update**, to start Microsoft Update, Figure 4-7.

   ▪ If a prompt appears asking to install and run Windows Update, click **Yes**.

   ▪ If a prompt appears saying that a new version of the Windows Update or Microsoft Update software is available, click on **Install Now** or **Download and Install Now** to install the new version. Multiple updates may be needed. If prompted to do so, close Internet Explorer or reboot the computer so that the new version of the update software takes effect. (If a reboot is needed, restart these instructions at step 1 after the reboot completes.)

3. Click on the **Custom** button to identify available updates.

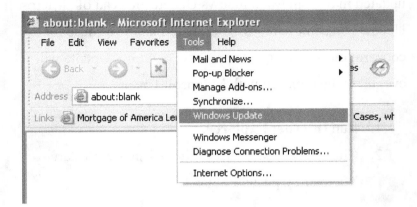

Figure 4-7 Windows Update option

The Custom option can install both high priority and optional updates, and allows the user to select which updates should be installed. The Express option can only install high priority updates, and does not allow the user to specify which updates should be installed. Using the Express option may cause the system to download and install service packs automatically.

Microsoft Update checks for updates and lists the available ones. The Figure 4-8 shows an example of how updates are listed. Depending on the service pack level of the Windows XP installation CD, either Service Pack 2 or non-service pack

updates should be displayed. Follow the
appropriate step:

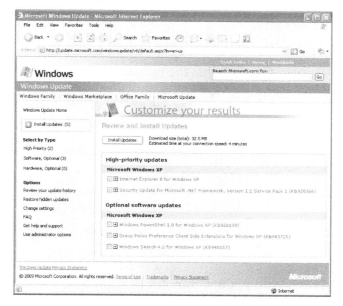

Figure 4-8 Microsoft Update website

A. **<u>Non-service pack updates</u>** are grouped by high
   priority updates, optional software updates, and
   optional hardware updates. High priority updates
   are defined as critical updates, hotfixes, service
   packs, and security rollups. Optional updates are
   unrelated to fixing security problems, but may
   contain new security features. Install them using
   the following steps:

   i.   Review the list of available updates, select the
        desired ones (or accept the default setting), then

click **Review and install updates**. In some cases, one patch may need to be installed by itself; therefore, it may not be possible to install all desired patches at once.

ii. Confirm that the correct updates are listed, and click the **Install Updates** button to perform the installations. Review any licensing agreements that are displayed and click on the appropriate button for each.

iii. The download and installation process will begin. Depending on the number of updates and the network bandwidth available, it may take from a few minutes to a few hours to download and install the updates. When the installations are done, Microsoft Update should report which updates were successfully installed. It will also prompt the user to reboot the computer if any of the updates require a reboot to complete the installation. Click on **OK** to reboot immediately or **Cancel** to manually reboot the computer later.

B. **Service Pack 2** can be installed through Microsoft Update using the following steps:

i. Select Service Pack 2.

ii. Click on **Download and Install Now**.

iii. Review the license agreement and click on the appropriate button.

Service Pack 2 should be downloaded and installed. This may take considerable time, depending primarily on the size of the service pack and the type of Internet connectivity and bandwidth available. The Windows XP Service Pack 2 Setup Wizard may prompt the user at some point; click **Next** to continue.

iv. Once the installation has ended, a summary should be displayed that reports the installation was successful. Click **Restart Now** to reboot the computer.

v. After the reboot, the **Help protect your PC** screen appears. The Automatic Updates setting is configured later in the instructions, so at this time, choose the **Not right now** option and click **Next**.

vi. The **Security Center** opens and displays the status of security programs. Since antivirus software and other security programs have not yet been installed on the computer, the current status is irrelevant. Close the **Security Center**.

C. **Service Pack 3** can be installed through Microsoft Update using the following steps:

   i.   Select Service Pack 3.
   ii.   Click on **Download and Install Now**.
   iii. Review the license agreement and click on the appropriate button.

   Service Pack 3 should be downloaded and installed. This may take considerable time, depending primarily on the size of the service pack and the type of Internet connectivity and bandwidth available. The Windows XP Service Pack 3 Setup Wizard may prompt the user at some point; click **Next** to continue.

   iv.   Once the installation has ended, a summary should be displayed that reports the installation was successful. Click **Restart Now** to reboot the computer.

4. Repeat all of these steps until no more updates are available. Depending on which service pack was included with the Windows XP CD, and the number of additional updates that need to be applied, it may take several rounds of updating the computer and rebooting it to bring a new Windows XP installation completely up-to-date.

During the updating process, the computer may state that additional updates cannot be downloaded until Windows XP has been validated or activated. If so, follow the instructions provided by Windows XP to activate the software through the Internet, dial-up, or telephone.

It is also important to update other applications on the Windows XP computer. Follow these steps for each application:

1. Install the application. It is often beneficial to install applications such as e-mail clients and web browsers before installing security software. For example, when antivirus software is installed, it may automatically identify installed email clients and configure itself so that it monitors their activity for malware.

2. Review its documentation for guidance on how to update it and how to configure it to update itself automatically (if possible).

3. Implement the vendor's recommendations. If needed, close and restart the application, or reboot the computer, so that the changes take effect.

Configure the Computer for Automatic Updates

To keep Windows XP fully updated at all times, it is highly recommended that the Automatic Updates service built in to Windows XP be enabled. This should keep both Windows XP and key Microsoft applications (e.g., Internet Explorer, Outlook Express) fully updated. To enable and configure Automatic Updates, perform the following steps:

1. From **Control Panel**, double-click **Automatic Updates**.

2. Choose the appropriate radio button, as shown below.

   - If the computer has high-speed Internet access, select **Automatic (recommended)**. Then select the frequency and timeframe in which the updates should be downloaded and installed (e.g., every day at 3:00 A.M.)

- If the computer has low-speed Internet access, select **Notify me but don't automatically download or install them**. This allows the user to control when updates are downloaded.

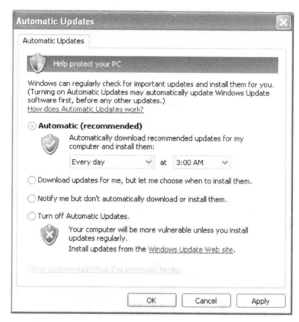

Figure 4-9 Automatic Updates window

3. Click on **OK** to save the Automatic Updates configuration.

Myth: Using either antivirus software or a firewall is a 100% effective solution for protecting my computer.

Truth: Antivirus software and firewalls are important tools for protecting a computer; however, neither technology by itself can provide complete protection. It is best to combine these technologies and use good security habits to reduce your overall risk.

Additional Security Steps

The next task in securing a new Windows XP computer is installing and configuring security software. Section 4.3 describes how to enable and configure a personal firewall to block unauthorized network access to the computer. This section provides guidance on configuring other types of software, such as antivirus software, web browser popup blocking, and content filtering programs, that can be effective at preventing malware infections and other types of attacks.

Malware Protection

After applying updates to the computer, users should next install malware protection utilities. Antivirus software is a necessity, and antispyware software is also recommended if the antivirus software does not include a robust antispyware capability. Install the antivirus software (and separate antispyware software, if needed) using the documentation provided with the software. During the software installation process, or immediately afterward, the software should be configured as follows, using directions provided within the software documentation:

✓ Scan critical operating system components such as startup files, memory, system BIOS, and boot records

✓ Perform real-time scans of each file as it is downloaded, opened, or executed

✓ Monitor common applications such as e-mail clients, Web browsers, file transfer and file sharing programs, and instant messaging software

✓ Scan all hard drives regularly (at least once a week)

✓ Attempt to disinfect files, and quarantine infected files that cannot be disinfected

✓ Automatically download and install updates daily.

After installation, the software should be fully updated. Consult the software documentation or help files for directions on how to download and install updates. Most antivirus software and antispyware software have a menu option that causes the software to check for, download, and install updates immediately. After doing so, it may be necessary to repeat the update process once or a few times, because some updates might need to be installed before other updates. Also, it may be necessary to reboot the computer after applying certain updates.

Content Filtering

Users may also want to use content filtering software, such as spam and web content filtering software. Some e-mail clients and web browsers have such capabilities built-in; they can also be performed by third-party software. Content filtering programs are helpful in stopping certain types of malware, but are not necessities. If content filtering is to be performed on the computer, install and configure the software using the documentation provided. The software should be configured to check for updates frequently and either to download and install updates automatically, or to let the user know when updates are available so that the user can download and install them at a convenient time.

After installation, the software should be fully updated. Consult the software documentation or help files for directions on how to download and install updates. Most content filtering programs or software features have a menu option that causes the software to check for, download, and install updates immediately. After doing so, it may be necessary to repeat the update process one or a few times, because some updates might need to be installed before other updates. Also, it may be necessary to reboot the computer after applying certain updates.

Personal Firewall

Section 4.3 provides instructions for enabling the Windows Firewall. Because third-party personal firewall programs may offer additional functionality, users may choose to disable Windows Firewall and use a third-party firewall instead. Only one personal firewall should be enabled on the computer at a time. Because a Windows XP computer should always have a personal firewall enabled when it is connected to a network, users who want to switch firewalls should first enable the second firewall and then immediately disable the first firewall. An alternative is to disconnect the computer from all networks, then disable the first firewall and enable the second firewall. This may be necessary if the second firewall cannot be enabled while the first firewall is still enabled.

To disable Windows Firewall, perform the following steps:

1. In the **Control Panel**, double-click on **Security Center**.
2. In the **Security Center**, choose to manage security settings for **Windows Firewall**.
3. Set the **Off** option, and then click **OK**.

4. Close the **Security Center**.

Users should configure the personal firewall to use the following settings whenever possible:

- Enable the personal firewall to protect every network interface on the computer, including wired and wireless networks cards, as well as dial-up access
- Only permit authorized activities; deny all others by default, or prompt the user to manually accept or reject each unknown activity. Prompting the user to make these decisions works best with users that have strong knowledge of software and security. Novice users are unlikely to understand the messages presented by the firewall, so they tend to allow unknown activity, which defeats the purpose of having the firewall. Accordingly, personal firewalls should be set to prompt the user only if it is reasonably certain that users will make the right decisions.
- Restrict both incoming and outgoing activity.

Myth: Since there is nothing important on my computer, I do not need to protect it.

Truth: Attackers can use any type of personal or financial information stored on your computer for their own financial gain. Even if you do not save any information on your computer, an attacker may be able to exploit vulnerabilities in your system and then use it to attack other people.

Customize Default Configuration

Once computer security programs have been installed and configured, the next step is to alter the Windows XP configuration to further improve security. This section recommends specific changes to the default Windows XP configuration.

User Accounts and Session

Whether a Windows XP computer has a single shared account or multiple accounts, each account usually should have a password. Without a password, unauthorized people could use the computer—not only people with physical access to the computer, but also possibly remote attackers contacting the computer through the Internet if the computer is not protected through a personal firewall and other technical controls. Windows XP does not have any requirements for the quality of passwords, such as minimum password length, so users are responsible for understanding the desirable characteristics of passwords and selecting sufficiently strong passwords. Recommended practices include the following:

Change User Account Password

To make the changes related to a user account, perform the following steps:

1. From the **Control Panel**, double-click on **User Accounts**.
2. Create strong passwords and safeguard them on password reset disks or paper for all administrator accounts. To do so, perform the following steps for each user account:

   A. Select a user account.
   B. Click **Create a password**.
   C. Enter a new password and type it once more to confirm it. Do not enter a password hint. Click the **Create Password** button.
   D. By default, the administrative account's files and folders are available to other users of the computer. To make them private, click on the **Yes, Make Private** button.
   E. If the computer has a floppy drive, perform the following steps:

      i. In the **Related Tasks** box, click on the **Prevent a forgotten password** link.

ii. The Forgotten Password Wizard should start. Click on **Next**.

iii. As directed, place a blank, formatted floppy disk into the drive and click **Next**.

iv. Enter the current administrative password and click **Next**.

v. The wizard creates the disk. When the creation is completed, click **Next**, and then click **Finish**.

vi. Store the password reset disk in a physically secure area, because anyone could use it to gain administrative access to the computer.

F. If the computer does not have a floppy drive, write the password for the administrative account on a piece of paper and store it securely, such as in a safe or lockbox.

Create a New User Account

For each person that will be using the computer, create a separate limited user account for daily use:

1. From the **Control Panel**, double-click on **User Accounts**.

2. Click **Create a new account**.

3. Enter the user name; it can be up to 20 characters long and contain letters, numbers, spaces, and some other types of punctuation. When finished, click the Next button.

4. Set the account type to **Limited**, and then click on the **Create Account** button.

5. Have the user choose a strong password and enter it after clicking **Create a password**. Ask the user not to enter a password hint.

Fast User Switching

Enabling the Fast User Switching feature allows two users to be logged on simultaneously without having access to each other's sessions. To enable the feature, perform these steps:

1. From the **Control Panel**, click on **User Accounts**.

2. Click on **Change the way users log on or off**.

3. Check the **Use the Welcome screen** and **Use Fast User Switching** options to enable the Welcome screen and FUS features.

4. Click on **Apply Options**.

5. Close the **User Accounts** window.

Secure Administrator Account

It is important to ensure that the default Administrator account has a password set. Because this account can only be accessed from Safe Mode, the computer needs to be rebooted to set the password. Perform the following steps:

1. Close all programs. From the **Start** menu, click **Turn Off Computer**, then click the **Restart** icon.

2. When the computer starts to reboot, hit the **F8** key on the keyboard to display the Windows Advanced Option Menu.

3. Choose **Safe Mode**, Figure 6-1, and hit the **Enter** key.

4. At the next screen, select **Microsoft Windows XP** and hit the **Enter** key. Various text messages should be displayed on the screen, and eventually the Windows XP logon screen should appear. The graphics and font sizes will appear slightly different; this is a characteristic of Safe Mode only, and the graphics and fonts will return to normal when the computer is rebooted regularly.

5. Log in as the **Administrator** user. If asked if the computer should be run in Safe Mode, choose **Yes**.

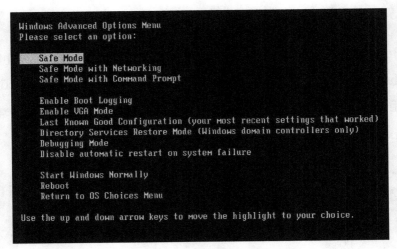

Figure 6-1 Windows Advanced Options Menu

6. Perform Steps 1 and 2 from the previous Change User Account Password section for the Administrator account. These steps will ensure that the default Administrator account has a password set and that if the password is forgotten, that access can still be gained through the physically secured copy of the password or the password reset disk.

7. Close the **User Accounts** window and the **Control Panel**.

8. From the **Start** menu, click **Turn Off Computer**, then click the **Restart** icon. The computer should reboot normally.

Disable Unneeded Networking Features

A Windows XP computer can be configured to limit network access; this can reduce the number of ways in which attackers can try to gain access to the computer. This section makes recommendations for configuring networking features to provide increased protection for the computer.

By default, Windows XP includes several networking features that can provide communications and data sharing between computers. Most computers do not need to use all of these features. Because many attacks are network-based, Windows XP computers should only use the necessary networking features, which should reduce the likelihood that the computer will be compromised or misused. On Windows XP computers, the networking features that are the most likely candidates for being disabled are as follows:

- The **Quality of Service (QoS) Packet Scheduler,** which is designed to prioritize network traffic by application over slow network connections. For example, it could give e-mail communications priority over Web surfing. Unfortunately, most applications cannot use the QoS feature, so the QoS Packet Scheduler is beneficial in very few home user situations.

- The **File and Printer Sharing for Microsoft Networks** service, which allows other computers to connect to the local computer's file and printer shares. This service should only be enabled on the computer if the computer shares files or printers with other computers, see Section 6.6, or if a particular application on the computer requires the service to be enabled. Disabling this service does not prevent users on the local computer from connecting to other computers' shared files and printers.

- The **Client for Microsoft Networks** service, which allows a Windows XP computer to use folders and printers that are shared by other computers on the local network. This service should only be enabled if the computer needs to access shared folders and printers, or if a particular application on the computer requires the service to be enabled. Disabling this service does not prevent the local computer from sharing its folders or printers with other computers on the local network.

The features mentioned above were disabled in Section 3.3, Installation Process. So no further action should be required.

Disable the use of remote access tools

The Remote Assistance (RA) feature of Windows XP provides a way to get remote technical support assistance from a coworker, friend, or family member when running into problems with a computer. Users in need of assistance can send an invitation to start an RA session through the Windows Messenger facility, e-mail requests, and via a Web e-mail service (filling out a form to request assistance). Unfortunately, if RA is configured improperly, unauthorized parties could use it to gain remote access to a computer. Therefore, RA should be disabled except when needed.

Some users also acquire third-party utilities that permit remote access to the computer from other computers. Although this may be convenient, it also increases the risk that the computer will be accessed by remote unauthorized parties. Therefore, such utilities should be enabled only when needed and configured to require authentication (e.g., username and password) before granting remote access.

Windows XP's Remote Assistance feature, as well as all third-party remote access tools installed on a Windows XP computer, should be disabled except when specifically needed. To disable the use of Remote Assistance, perform the following steps:

1. From the **Control Panel**, double-click the **System** icon.

   The System Properties window should appear.

2. Click the **Remote** tab.

3. Uncheck **Allow Remote Assistance invitations to be sent from this computer**.

4. Click **OK**.

Secure wireless networking

Wireless networking transfers information through the air between a user's computer and a device known as a wireless access point (AP). If improperly configured, wireless networking can cause sensitive information to be transmitted without adequate protection, exposing it to others in close geographic proximity.

If the computer uses wireless networking, review the documentation provided with the wireless access point and the computer's wireless network card, and then implement the following recommendations according to the vendor directions. These directions assume that the Microsoft wireless management utility is being used, not a third-party utility provided by the computer's vendor or the wireless network card's vendor. If a third-party utility is being used, do **not** follow the directions in this section; instead, consult the vendor's directions for additional guidance on secure configuration.

WEP, wired equivalent privacy, uses a series of letters, digits, and other characters to create a key that is used to limit access to wireless networks. A wireless access point can be configured to require all computers attempting to connect to it to use a WEP key. When a computer attempts to join the wireless network, it must provide the same WEP key as the one stored in the access point. Users should set a WEP key that is long and complex, making it hard for others to guess. This should help to prevent people in close physical proximity to the access point from gaining unauthorized access to the wireless network.

To provide a better solution for wireless security, an industry group called the Wi-Fi Alliance has created a series of product certifications called Wi-Fi Protected Access (WPA), which include the WPA1 and WPA2 certifications. Computers with wireless network cards that support either WPA1 or WPA2 can use their security features, such as using Advanced Encryption Security (AES) for encrypting network communications. Whenever available, users should choose 128-bit encryption or greater.

Note: If the wireless access point or the wireless network card is a few years old, it may not support the newer WPA standards.

1. Create a long and complex key.
2. Configure the wireless access point so the encryption key is required. Enter it into the wireless access point and the Windows XP computer. To do the latter, go to Section 4.4 or perform the following steps:

   A. From the **Control Panel**, double-click **Network Connections**.
   B. Right-click on the wireless network connection configuration and select **Properties**.
   C. Click on the **Wireless Networks** tab. Highlight the correct wireless network in the **Preferred Networks** list and click the **Properties** button. Below is an example of the security configuration settings that need to be made.

Figure 6-2 Wireless Network Properties window

D. Set **Data encryption** to the highest possible setting that both the wireless access point and the Windows XP wireless network card can use. The encryption choices will vary depending on the wireless network card. Recommended choices, in order with the most highly preferred option first, are as follows:

   i.   WPA2 with AES. To use WPA2 with Windows XP, the Windows XP Hot Fix KB893357 will need to be installed first.

   ii. WPA1 with AES

iii.   WPA1 with TKIP

iv.   WEP with 128-bit encryption.

Remember to configure the access point to use the same selected data encryption option. Consult the access point manufacturer's documentation for information on how to do this.

E. Clear the check box labeled **The key is provided for me automatically**.

F. Set the **Network authentication** to **Open**. Enter the WEP key in the **Network key** and **Confirm network key** boxes.

G. Click **OK** to save the changes, then click **OK** to close the wireless network connection properties window. Close the **Network Connections** window.

3. On the Windows XP computer, configure Wireless Auto Configuration so that it will not attempt to join any wireless network automatically and it will only connect to wireless access points. To do so, perform the following steps:

A. From **Control Panel**, double-click **Network Connections**.

B. Right-click on the wireless network connection configuration and select **Properties**.

C. Click on the **Wireless Networks** tab. Click the **Advanced** button in the lower right-hand corner.

D. Select the option labeled **Access point (infrastructure) networks only**. If the computer will be participating in ad hoc wireless networks (such as a peer-to-peer network with another computer), select the **Any available network (access point preferred)** option instead of **Access point (infrastructure) networks only**.

E. Clear the check box labeled **Automatically connect to non-preferred networks**, and then click **Close**.

F. Remove any networks from the Preferred Networks list that the computer should not be using.

G. Click **OK** to close the wireless network connection properties window. Close the **Network Connections** window.

4. Review the wireless access point's documentation. If it permits access to be restricted by the media access control (MAC) addresses of wireless network cards, enter the MAC addresses of all authorized wireless devices into the access point. To identify the MAC

address for a wireless network card on a Windows XP computer, perform the following steps:

A. From **Control Panel**, double-click **Network Connections**.

B. Double-click on the wireless network connection configuration.

C. Click the **Support** tab, then the **Details...** button.

D. The value listed for the **Physical Address** is the MAC address. It should be displayed in the format XX-XX-XX-XX-XX-XX, where each X is a digit or a letter in the range A to F. Write down the MAC address.

E. Click **Close**, then **Close**. Close the **Network Connections** window.

Configure ICS

Internet Connection Sharing (ICS) allows a Windows XP computer to share an Internet connection with other computers. ICS is most often used in SOHO environments when Internet access is available only through a dial-up modem in one computer. In such a situation, ICS can allow multiple computers to share the limited Internet connectivity. If a higher-bandwidth network is in use, such as DSL or cable modem service, it is generally easier to purchase an inexpensive router or other network hardware device and use it to share access among multiple computers. This allows each computer to access the Internet independently without relying on another computer running ICS, and reduces the burden on the computer that would have been running ICS.

If the computer uses dial-up networking to access the Internet, and other computers on the same home network need to share that Internet access, then it may be necessary to enable ICS. Otherwise, ICS should be disabled. To configure ICS properly, perform the following steps:

1. From the **Control Panel**, select **Network Connections**.
2. Right-click on the network connection with Internet access and select **Properties**, Figure 6-3.
3. Click on the **Advanced** tab.
4. Perform the appropriate step based on the need for ICS:

    If ICS is not needed, disable it by clearing the check box labeled **Allow other network users to connect through this computer's Internet connection**.

    ▪ **If ICS is needed**, check the item labeled **Allow other network users to connect through this computer's Internet connection**. Then, uncheck the item labeled

Allow other network users to control or disable the shared Internet connection.

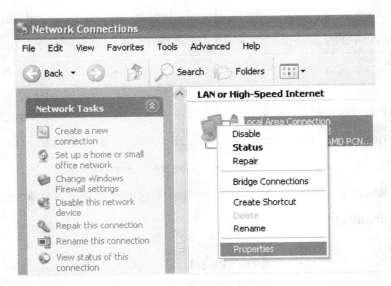

Figure 6-3 Local Area Connection Properties option

If ICS is used, the computer running ICS should use a personal firewall such as Windows Firewall. Not only can the firewall provide protection for the ICS computer, but it can also help to protect the computers behind the ICS from attacks by external parties. Although ICS can provide network address translation (NAT) services to other computers, which essentially hide them from public view, NAT cannot protect computers against many types of threats.

5. Click on **OK**, and then close the **Network Connections** window.

Sharing Files and Folders

The Shared Folders feature of Windows XP causes folders called Shared Documents and Shared Pictures to be accessible by all users on the computer, but not remote users. This allows users to share files without sharing user accounts or permitting other users to access their personal folders. Unfortunately, Shared Folders cannot be configured to limit access to some users; all users can read and modify all files in the shared folders. If more restrictive sharing is needed, such as permitting all users to read but not modify files, users should create their own folders and share them. A disadvantage of using a custom share is that it cannot be set up for just local users of the computer; it must also be available to users on other computers across the network.

The following steps describe how to configure file and folder sharing that permits read-only access, perform the following steps:

1. Open **My Computer** and right-click the folder that should be shared, and click on the **Sharing and Security...** option.

2. Click on the link labeled **If you understand the security risks but want to share files without running the wizard, click here**, Figure 6-4.

3. Select the **Just enable file sharing** option and click **OK**.

4. To share the folder with users on other computers, check the **Share this folder on the network** box and enter a name (or use the default name) for the share in the **Share name** box. Uncheck the **Allow network users to change my files** box so that users can read but not modify the files.

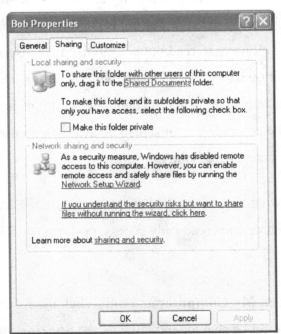

Figure 6-4 Network sharing and security

5. Click **OK.**

If the Shared Documents folder needs to be made available to users on other computers of the local network, perform the following steps:

1. Open **My Computer** and right-click the **Shared Documents** folder. Click on the **Sharing and Security...** option.

2. Check the **Share this folder on the network** box. Enter a name (or use the default name) for the share in the **Share name** box. If network users should be able to read and modify the shared files, check the **Allow network users to change my files** box, otherwise uncheck it.

3. Click **OK.**

Myth: After I install software on my computer, I do not have to concern myself about it anymore.

Truth: Vendors usually release patches to fix problems or vulnerabilities in their software. You should routinely check help to ensure your computer is running as stable and securely as possible. vendors' websites for patches that apply to both the operating system and installed applications. Installing these patches will

Restore Files and Settings

The final step in the Windows XP installation process is to restore previously backed up data files and configuration settings, if needed. Data files should not be restored until antivirus software and antispyware software has been installed, updated fully, and configured to scan all files, in case the backup media contains any malware or spyware.

When restoring settings from backups, users should be very careful about overwriting existing settings on the computer. For example, old application settings may be insecure; restoring them onto the computer could inadvertently affect the security of the application, which in turn could reduce the security profile of the computer. Users should also be aware of differences in directory structures; some versions of Windows have used different directories for holding files. Consequently, it may be necessary to restore file backups to different directories so that files are in the proper locations.

To restore data files or configuration settings that were backed up using the directions in Sections 2.2 – 2.6, perform the following steps:

1. Retrieve the media that contains the backup.
2. Transfer the files and settings from the media to the Windows XP computer using the chosen method:

Backup or Restore Wizard

1. Go to **Start**, then **All Programs**, and choose **Accessories**. Next, select **System Tools**, and click on the **Backup** icon. This should launch the Backup or Restore Wizard.
2. Click the **Next** button. Select **Restore files and settings**, Figure 7-1, then click the **Next** button.

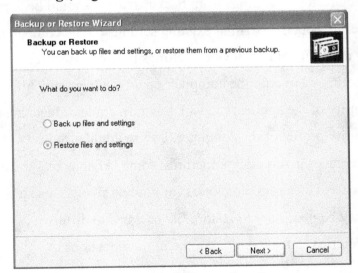

Figure 7-1 Restore files and settings

3. The **What to Restore** window appears, Figure 7-2, asking the user which backup file to restore. Select the backup file to restore and click the **Next** button.

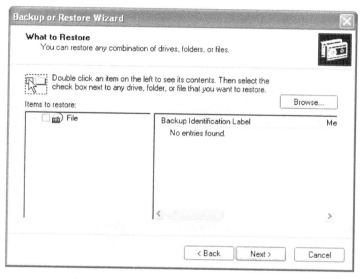

Figure 7-2 What to Restore window

Files and Settings Transfer Wizard

1. Click on **Start**, then **All Programs**. Choose **Accessories**, then **System Tools**. Select the **Files and Settings Transfer Wizard**, and then click **Next**.

2. Select **New computer**, Figure 7-3, to restore the previously captured files and settings, and then click **Next**.

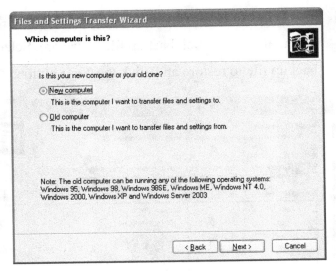

Figure 7-3 Which computer is this screen

3. Choose the **I don't need the Wizard Disk** option, Figure 7-4, since the backup was already performed, then click **Next**.

4. When prompted for the location of the files and settings, choose **Other**, Figure 7-5, and select the location of the backup. Then click **Next**.

5. The wizard restores the files and settings. When it is done, click **Finished**. The computer may need to be rebooted before the new settings take effect.

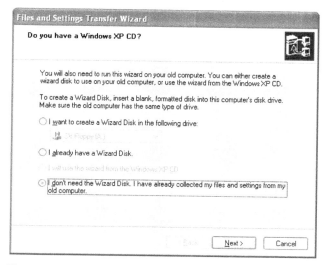

Figure 7-4 Do you have a Windows XP CD window

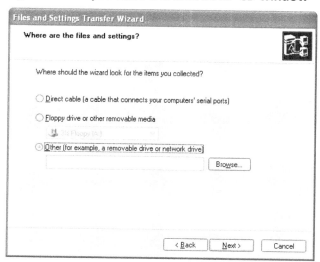

Figure 7-5 Where are the files and settings window

Third-Party Backup and Restore Utility

Run the utility and perform the restore based on the utility vendor's documentation.

Third-Party Remote Backup Service

Perform the restore using the remote backup service's software and directions.

File Copy to Media

Select the files on the media to be restored, and drag them onto the appropriate folder on the Windows XP computer. Alternately, copy the files to be restored, and paste them into the appropriate folder. Perform this as many times as needed to restore all the preserved files.

Summary

A new Windows XP computer should be secured properly before it is used or connected to a network to minimize the possibility of a security breach. As a first step, users should perform preparatory actions, including gathering needed materials, setting the default view for Control Panel, and identifying the Windows XP service pack currently in use. The next step is to apply updates to the computer. Before doing this, a personal firewall needs to be set up on the computer to block malicious activity from other computers. Until the computer has been fully updated, applications such as e-mail clients should not be used; the only application use should be that which is required to update the computer or configure the personal firewall. Microsoft Update provides a convenient way to identify, download, and install updates for Windows XP and selected Microsoft applications. Windows XP computers should also be configured to use the built-in Automatic Updates feature, which helps to keep the computer up-to-date.

After completing the updating process, the next step in securing a Windows XP computer is installing and configuring additional security software. Antivirus software is a necessity; antispyware software should also be installed if the antivirus software does not include a robust antispyware capability. Users may also want to use content filtering software, such as spam and Web content filtering software, and a third-party personal firewall.

Once security software has been installed and configured, the next step is to alter the Windows XP configuration to further improve security. This includes creating separate password-protected user accounts for each person, securing networking features, protecting temporary files, and configuring folder sharing.

The overall security of a Windows XP computer should be improved once all recommendations have completed in this guide.

Resources

Full Featured Antivirus/Antimalware Software

- VIPRE Antivirus (http://viprediscount.com/)

Free Antivirus/Antimalware software

- Ad-Aware (http://www.lavasoft.com/)
- AVG Anti-Virus (http://free.avg.com/)

Product Key Finder

- Jalapeño Keyfinder (http://www.jalapenosoftware.com/)

Online Backup Service

- Carbonite (http://carbonite.com/)
- Mozy (http://mozy.com/)